RELATIONSHIPS & CONSENT

by
John Wood

BookLife
PUBLISHING

©2018
BookLife Publishing
King's Lynn
Norfolk PE30 4LS

All rights reserved.
Printed in Malaysia.

A catalogue record for this
book is available from the
British Library.

ISBN: 978-1-78637-383-0

Written by:
John Wood

Edited by:
Holly Duhig

Designed by:
Danielle Rippengill

CONTENTS

Words that look like **this** can be found in the glossary on page 31.

WHAT IS A RELATIONSHIP?

There are many people in your life. You might have parents, siblings, family, friends and teachers. Some people talk to you every day, and you might know them very well. You might only see other people now and then, and so you will talk to them differently. The way you interact with someone and the type of **connection** you have is called a relationship. There are many different types of relationships, and some are stronger than others.

WHY DO WE NEED RELATIONSHIPS?

It doesn't matter whether you love to talk or whether you are very shy, we all need some strong relationships in our lives. People are **social**, and they need to work together and **support** each other. A good relationship can calm us down when we are angry or scared, or it can cheer us up when we are down. Nobody wants to be alone all the time, and it would be very hard to go through your day with nobody to talk to, or nobody to help you.

CAN YOU THINK OF DIFFERENT PEOPLE WHO HELP YOU, OR PEOPLE THAT YOU TALK TO EVERY DAY?

4

HEALTHY AND UNHEALTHY RELATIONSHIPS

Relationships can be healthy or unhealthy. A healthy relationship is one where both people feel good because they treat each other fairly and kindly. People in healthy relationships work together, help each other or enjoy being around one another. However, some relationships can be unhealthy. In an unhealthy relationship, people might argue all the time, or they might hurt each other a lot. You might also feel **ignored** or even unsafe in an unhealthy relationship.

HEALTHY RELATIONSHIPS MAKE YOU FEEL GOOD.

UNHEALTHY RELATIONSHIPS MAKE YOU FEEL BAD.

Sometimes it is hard to know when a relationship is unhealthy. Some relationships can seem healthy when we are in them, but are actually not healthy. Other people might see this before we do. Sometimes we can be the cause of a problem without realising it. However, we can recognise and change an unhealthy relationship by talking to each other and listening to what other people say. This makes it easier to know if everyone is being treated how they want to be treated.

TYPES OF RELATIONSHIPS

PARENTS, CARERS AND TEACHERS

You will have many different relationships with adults. For example, you have a different kind of relationship with your parent or carer than you do with the teachers at school. You may know other adults who are part of your family, or friends of your parents or carer.

In many of these relationships, the adult needs to look after you and help you. This often means they have to tell you what to do. It is important to follow the rules and do what they say, as long as it is safe to do so.

IN A HEALTHY RELATIONSHIP, AN ADULT SHOULD ALWAYS MAKE YOU FEEL SAFE. IF THEY DON'T MAKE YOU FEEL SAFE, SPEAK TO ANOTHER ADULT ABOUT IT.

IF OUR FRIENDS ASK US TO HELP THEM, WE CAN CHOOSE TO DO IT TO BE KIND.

FRIENDS

You probably have relationships with people your age too. You might have friends at school, or siblings or cousins in your family who are the same age as you. This is not like a relationship with an adult because friends and other children should treat each other equally. In any kind of relationship, you don't have to do what someone tells you to do if you think it's wrong or unkind.

ROMANTIC RELATIONSHIPS

Two people from different families might live together if they love each other. This is called a romantic relationship. A romantic relationship involves more **affectionate** and **physical** things, such as kissing and hugging. A person in a romantic relationship might be called a partner, girlfriend, or boyfriend. Together they might be called a couple. They might have children together or they might not. Healthy romantic relationships are often long-term, and the couple are honest, open, and always help each other.

PROFESSIONAL RELATIONSHIPS

A professional is someone who gets paid to do something. You have probably met some people in professional positions, such as postal workers or caretakers. You will have a professional relationship with these people. This kind of relationship isn't personal, and mostly doesn't go beyond the work that the professional is doing. For example, when you go to see your dentist, you will mostly talk about your teeth. When the check-up is over and you leave, you probably won't see your dentist again until the next check-up.

DOCTORS ARE PROFESSIONALS WHOM YOU ONLY TALK TO WHEN YOU ARE ILL.

WHAT IS CONSENT?

If you are going to do something that affects someone else, you should ask their permission. This is especially true when it comes to our bodies, our **personal boundaries** and our private lives. For example, if you wanted to read someone's diary, you would have to ask them first. If they give you permission by clearly saying 'yes', it is called giving you consent. Once you have their consent, you may read the diary. However, they might say no, or say nothing. This means you do not have their consent. It is wrong to do something that affects somebody else's boundaries if you don't have their consent.

GIVING OR NOT GIVING CONSENT IS AN IMPORTANT SIGNAL THAT SOMEONE CAN USE IF THEY FEEL **INTIMIDATED** AND UNABLE TO SPEAK UP.

WHY IS CONSENT IMPORTANT?

Getting someone's consent before doing something that affects their personal boundaries will make them feel safe. In some relationships, people can be shy about saying how they truly feel. Asking for consent means that people can always say what they are comfortable with.

CONSENT IS IMPORTANT IN ALL SORTS OF RELATIONSHIPS, INCLUDING ROMANTIC ONES.

IT IS OK FOR PEOPLE TO CHANGE THEIR MIND ABOUT CONSENT.

PEOPLE CAN CHANGE THEIR MIND

Sometimes, people say yes to something, but then decide against it and say no afterwards. This means you do not have their consent anymore. It doesn't matter if someone said yes before; all that matters is how they feel now. If you are not sure how they feel, and even if they are not sure how they feel, this means that you still don't have their consent.

For example, imagine you want to visit a friend's house. Your friend might want to be alone, but they might not know how to say no without sounding mean. By asking for permission, you won't accidentally overstep any personal boundaries, and your friend will know you **respect** them and their privacy.

Now imagine you are playing a wrestling game with a friend or a sibling. Wrestling is a very physical game. Sometimes your friend wants to play wrestling but then changes their mind. Part of respecting people's personal boundaries is listening to them when they say they don't want to play anymore. If they change their mind about playing, then they are no longer giving consent.

WHO NEEDS CONSENT?

When it comes to your body and your personal boundaries, everyone needs consent. Everyone has a different idea about what is OK and not OK when it comes to their own bodies and their personal boundaries. It is up to each of us to decide what we are comfortable with. Once we have decided what we are happy with, everyone must respect that decision.

TRUSTED ADULTS AND CONSENT

Your relationship with a trusted adult, like a parent, carer or teacher, is different to other relationships. Parents and carers will often tell you what to do, and they make lots of decisions for you. For example, parents or carers will tell you what time you have to go to bed, or what you have to eat for dinner. However, they do these things to look after you, or to keep you healthy. This is not the same as forcing you to do something that makes you uncomfortable or unsafe. However, when it comes to very personal things, like touching your body, adults still need your consent too.

PARENTS AND CARERS ALSO GIVE DOCTORS PERMISSION TO GIVE YOU TREATMENT IF YOU ARE ILL.

Sometimes it is easy to know what is right and wrong when it comes to your body and your personal boundaries. For example, nobody likes being hit, or to have someone yelling in their face. These things are wrong, and they definitely cross your personal boundaries. But other things might be different for different people. For example, some children like being tickled. They might like being tickled by their parents, but not like being tickled by their friends.

Below is a list of things to think about. Which of these are you comfortable with? Are there situations or people that would make you uncomfortable with these things? There is no right or wrong answer to these questions – you are free to decide what is OK and what is not OK when it comes to your body and personal boundaries.

HUGGING AND KISSING TO SAY HELLO OR GOODBYE

WRESTLING

PUTTING AN ARM AROUND EACH OTHER

SITTING CLOSELY TOGETHER

BEING PICKED UP

11

CLOTHES AND PRIVACY

In most countries around the world, people wear clothes to cover up their bodies. This is to keep warm, but also because some parts of our bodies are very private. As you grow up and your body changes, it is normal to want more privacy than you did when you were younger. Your body belongs to you and nobody else, and it is very normal to keep it private from most of the people that you know.

Some parts of the body are more private than others. Some parts are very private, such as your **genitals** or your bottom. We wear clothes in front of other people and go to the bathroom alone in order to keep these parts private. When we are much younger, very trusted adults like our parents might help us with things such as washing, getting changed or going to the toilet.

A BATHROOM IS A PRIVATE PLACE.

CHANGING BODIES AND CHANGING CONSENT

As we grow older, we might want to keep our bodies more private, and even very trusted people, like parents, need your permission before they touch private parts of your body. It is important to talk to your parents or carers about this and be honest and open about what makes you comfortable.

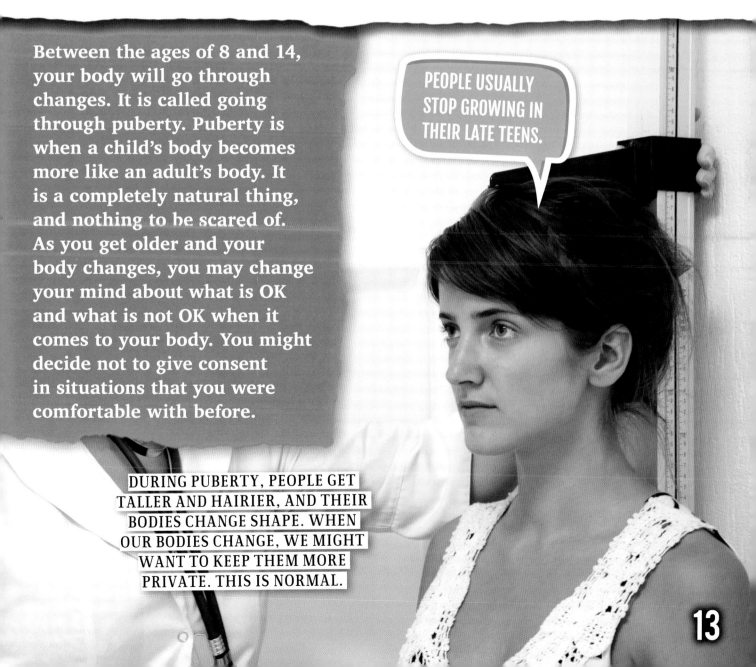

Between the ages of 8 and 14, your body will go through changes. It is called going through puberty. Puberty is when a child's body becomes more like an adult's body. It is a completely natural thing, and nothing to be scared of. As you get older and your body changes, you may change your mind about what is OK and what is not OK when it comes to your body. You might decide not to give consent in situations that you were comfortable with before.

PEOPLE USUALLY STOP GROWING IN THEIR LATE TEENS.

DURING PUBERTY, PEOPLE GET TALLER AND HAIRIER, AND THEIR BODIES CHANGE SHAPE. WHEN OUR BODIES CHANGE, WE MIGHT WANT TO KEEP THEM MORE PRIVATE. THIS IS NORMAL.

THINKING OF OTHERS

SEEKING CONSENT

We must always look for other people's permission and consent in our relationships. Remember, it is never OK to do something that affects someone's personal boundaries without consent, even if it part of a game. We should ask for consent in all sorts of situations. For example, when playing a game with friends, we need to check that everyone wants to play so we aren't forcing someone to do something that they don't want to.

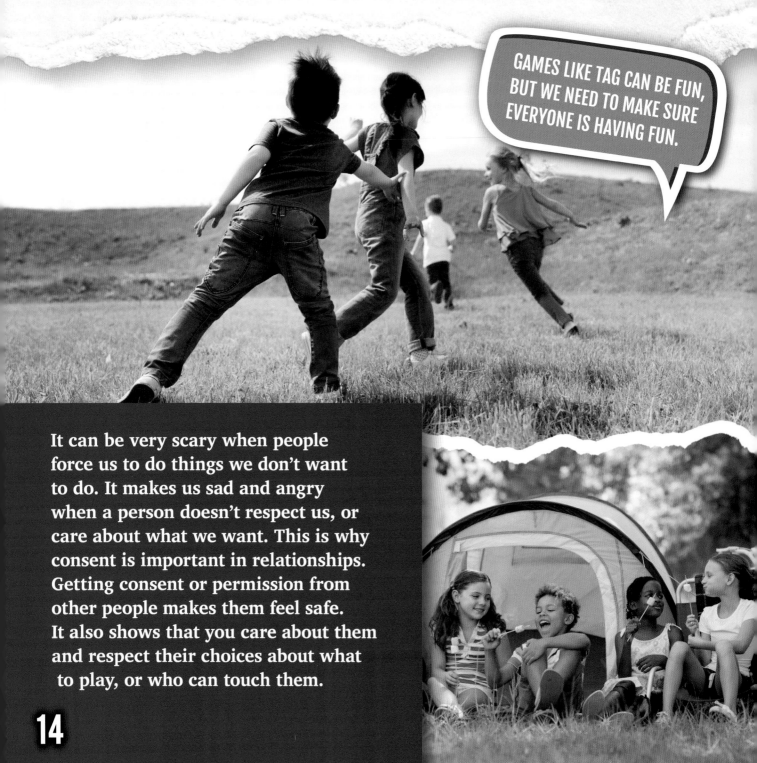

GAMES LIKE TAG CAN BE FUN, BUT WE NEED TO MAKE SURE EVERYONE IS HAVING FUN.

It can be very scary when people force us to do things we don't want to do. It makes us sad and angry when a person doesn't respect us, or care about what we want. This is why consent is important in relationships. Getting consent or permission from other people makes them feel safe. It also shows that you care about them and respect their choices about what to play, or who can touch them.

UNDERSTANDING THE
FEELINGS OF OTHERS

Asking for consent isn't always straightforward. A person might feel like they aren't allowed to say no, or they might be too shy or scared to say anything at all. If somebody says nothing, it does not mean that they give you consent. Sometimes people might say yes, even though they don't want to. However, there are other ways to tell how someone is really feeling.

BODY LANGUAGE

The way someone moves, or how they stand or sit, can show you how they are feeling. This is called body language, and people often do it without thinking.

For example, someone might make themselves look small by drooping their head or hunching their shoulders. This might mean they and are scared and trying to hide.

FACIAL EXPRESSIONS

We use facial expressions to show emotions. A smile is a facial expression which usually means someone feels happy, while a frown or wide eyes might mean someone is angry or scared. It is important to watch people's facial expressions and body language when asking for consent to decide how they are really feeling.

FOLDED ARMS OR FIDGETING MIGHT MEAN SOMEONE IS UNCOMFORTABLE OR NERVOUS.

HOW DO YOU THINK THIS GIRL IS FEELING?

15

WHAT MAKES A
RELATIONSHIP HEALTHY?

HONESTY

Being honest and talking about our feelings can help other people to understand us better. If we do not **communicate**, people will never know what is bothering us. This makes it impossible to change or improve the relationship. Being honest doesn't mean just saying whatever you want – this could hurt people's feelings. When being honest, we must choose our words carefully. When telling a loved one or a friend that they said something upsetting, you could remind them that you still care about them a lot.

WHEN YOU LIE TO SOMEONE, IT CAN MAKE IT VERY HARD FOR THEM TO TRUST YOU NEXT TIME.

TRUST

When we trust someone, we feel safe in the knowledge that they will try to help us and do the right thing, and we will do the same for them. Trust and honesty are closely linked. If we trust someone, it means we are not scared of how they will react to our thoughts and feelings. This means we can be honest with them, and they will understand us better.

RESPECT

People must respect each other in a healthy relationship. If someone isn't respected, it means they won't be treated how they deserve to be treated. If someone isn't kind, you could try to be honest with them about what they are doing wrong. If you are careful about how you say it, and treat them with respect, they are more likely to change their ways. This could create a healthy relationship between you and that person.

WORKING TOGETHER

In a healthy relationship, people are always working together. You might be working together for different reasons, depending on the relationship. For example, you and your friends work together to play games and have as much fun as possible! You and your teacher work together so that you learn in a way that suits you. Most relationships are complicated, and there are many reasons why you work together and support each other.

RESPECT IS IMPORTANT WHEN TALKING TO ADULTS.

RELATIONSHIPS AROUND YOU

MARRIAGE

Marriage is a type of relationship where two adults **legally** recognise their romantic relationship. Being married is a type of relationship where people love each other and are affectionate. In many countries, marriage can be between anyone, whether that is a man and a woman, two men, or two women. Both people must consent to a marriage, and it is illegal to force anyone into a marriage. Some parents are married and have children. Other parents may choose not to be married. This doesn't mean they don't love each other, it just means they have chosen a different kind of relationship which they are comfortable with.

A MARRIED MAN IS CALLED A HUSBAND AND A MARRIED WOMAN IS CALLED A WIFE. A MARRIAGE OFTEN STARTS WITH A RELIGIOUS CEREMONY CALLED A WEDDING.

MARRIAGE IS MEANT TO LAST FOREVER. HOWEVER, SOMETIMES PEOPLE LEGALLY END THE MARRIAGE AND SPLIT UP THE RELATIONSHIP. THIS IS CALLED GETTING A DIVORCE.

CHILDREN DO NOT GET MARRIED UNTIL THEY ARE MUCH OLDER. IN MOST COUNTRIES, YOU MUST BE AROUND 16 OR 17 TO GET MARRIED.

CIVIL PARTNERSHIPS

A civil partnership is like a marriage, but it is not religious. Some people choose to have a civil partnership instead of a marriage because they do not like the **traditions** in marriage. Some people don't want to be in a marriage or a civil partnership.

RELATIONSHIPS IN ART AND THE MEDIA

Social media, films, video games, books and the news are all examples of art and the media. There are often lots of **unrealistic** examples of relationships, especially romantic ones. For example, films and TV rarely show romantic relationships between two women, or between two men. We usually only see marriages between men and women, which is unrealistic. TV programmes often show relationships where couples hurt each other, perfect relationships where people are never cross or upset, or old-fashioned relationships where the man is in charge and the woman has to do what he says. This is because TV programmes are made to be **dramatic** so people watch them. Relationships are rarely like this in the real world.

PEOPLE ONLY SHOW ONE SIDE OF THEIR RELATIONSHIPS ON SOCIAL MEDIA. THIS CAN GIVE AN UNREALISTIC IDEA OF WHAT THEIR RELATIONSHIPS ARE LIKE.

The media can make people feel like they need to be in grown-up romantic relationships and behave in a certain way. However, we do not need to copy what we see in these relationships, because the things we watch and read don't always show what relationships are actually like. It is important not to rush into anything because of something we see online, on TV or on social media.

RELATIONSHIPS DO NOT HAVE TO BE LIKE THOSE IN ART AND THE MEDIA; THE ONLY THING THAT MATTERS IS THAT BOTH PEOPLE ARE HAPPY.

SECRETS AND DARES

SECRETS

A secret is something that is kept hidden, and is not supposed to be told to anyone. Some secrets are fun, like a surprise birthday party. However, secrets can be bad too. Bad secrets hurt people, or make them feel worried or unsafe. If you are keeping a secret, it is important to think about whether it is a good secret or a bad secret. If it is a bad secret, you should tell a trusted adult what it is. If it would be unsafe to keep a secret, you are allowed to tell someone, even if you promised you wouldn't.

WHAT MAKES A SECRET BAD?

Here are some examples of bad secrets that you should tell an adult about:

- If someone touches you or someone else without consent and tells you to keep it a secret
- If someone has hurt or bullied you
- If it worries you
- If keeping the secret will hurt another person
- If someone has broken a rule or a law, or done something wrong
- If it makes you feel unsafe

SOMEONE MIGHT DARE YOU TO GO REALLY HIGH ON THE SWING. IF YOU FEEL IT IS UNSAFE, YOU DON'T HAVE TO DO THE DARE.

DARES

A dare is a game where someone tells you to do something risky or embarrassing, and you have to do it because they dared you to do it. Dares can be fun, but sometimes dares are bad. If you think that a dare is bad, you do not have to do it. Even if you agreed to play and have already dared other people to do things, you can still decide not to do a dare.

BAD DARES

Here are some examples of bad dares:
- A dare that physically hurts another person, or upsets them with words
- A dare that involves touching another person or overstepping their personal boundaries without their consent
- A dare that breaks rules or laws
- A dare that causes you to worry
- A dare that could hurt you
- A dare that you think might be unsafe

FEELINGS AND CONSENT

Sometimes it can be hard to say no. Sometimes people feel forced to give consent when they don't want to.

GUILT

Guilt is the feeling people get when they have done something wrong and feel bad about it. When someone feels guilty, they might feel hot and sweaty, they might have a nauseous feeling in their stomach, or they might feel restless. People feel guilty after they hurt someone, or break the rules.

However, sometimes we feel guilty when we haven't done anything wrong. If someone asks for our consent, we might feel guilty about saying no. We might feel like we are being mean or disappointing someone. However, there is no need to feel guilty. It is always fine to say no when it comes to your body. Nobody has a right to do something to your body without your permission.

IF SOMEONE WANTS TO KISS YOU GOODBYE, YOU MIGHT FEEL GUILTY SAYING NO. HOWEVER, THERE IS NO NEED TO FEEL GUILTY.

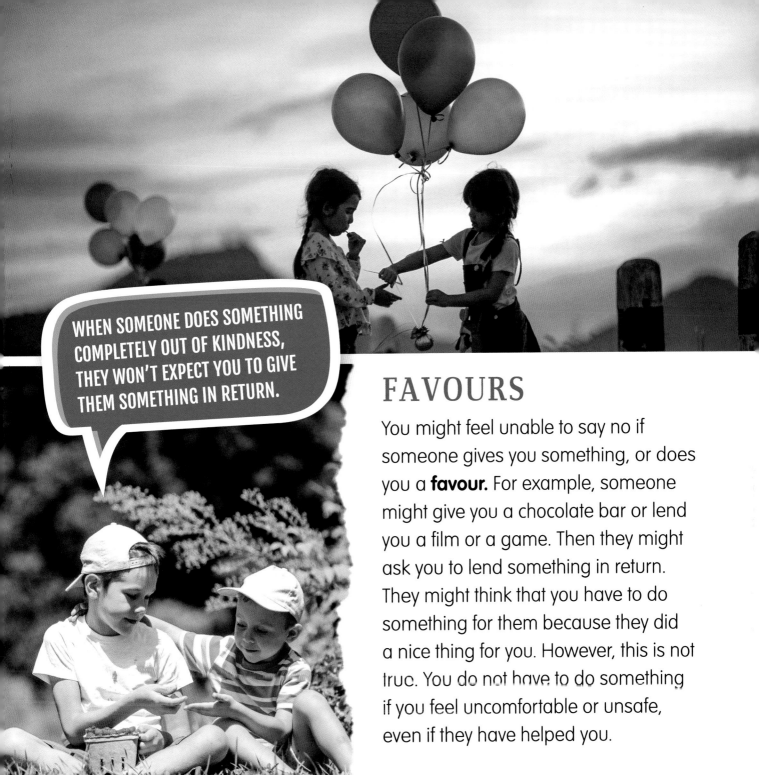

WHEN SOMEONE DOES SOMETHING COMPLETELY OUT OF KINDNESS, THEY WON'T EXPECT YOU TO GIVE THEM SOMETHING IN RETURN.

FAVOURS

You might feel unable to say no if someone gives you something, or does you a **favour.** For example, someone might give you a chocolate bar or lend you a film or a game. Then they might ask you to lend something in return. They might think that you have to do something for them because they did a nice thing for you. However, this is not true. You do not have to do something if you feel uncomfortable or unsafe, even if they have helped you.

It is nice to get a reward for following the rules or being good. However, being nice to people doesn't always earn you a reward, and that's OK. Helping people is about making them feel good, or solving a problem. Helping someone does not mean that you deserve whatever you want in return. In a healthy relationship, we do good things and work together because we like each other. It would be an unhealthy relationship if a person felt forced to say yes to anything they didn't want to do.

BULLYING AND RELATIONSHIPS

Everyone is different. There are lots of little things that make up who we are. This is called our identity. Our identity is made up of all sorts of things like:

– The country we live in
– What our family is like
– How old we are
– What religion we believe in, if any
– What our hobbies are
– What we like and dislike
– Whether you are male or female – this is called your sex
– Whether you feel like a boy, a girl or neither – this is called your gender

Having differences is a good thing because it makes people interesting to meet and talk to. It would be no fun if every person was the same. However, some people are bullied for their differences. Bullying is when someone uses strength or power to be mean or **violent** to someone else, usually over a long period of time. Bullying is wrong, and it makes people upset and unhappy.

TYPES OF BULLYING

Bullying might be physical. Bullies might hurt people by hitting them or grabbing them violently. However, bullying can be done with words too. Bullies might make people upset by saying mean things about them, spreading lies about them or never letting them join in games or **conversations**. Bullying is often long-term – it might happen every month, every week, or even every day.

BULLYING CAN HAPPEN BETWEEN CHILDREN OF THE SAME AGE. CHILDREN ARE SOMETIMES BULLIED BY OLDER PEOPLE TOO.

Bullying can happen online. People may post nasty comments or posts about someone. This is called cyberbullying, and is often **anonymous**. Trolling is another form of online bullying. This is where people will say and do things just to make someone angry, even if they don't really believe what they are saying.

BULLYING IS NOT HEALTHY. IT CAN MAKE SOMEONE FEEL SAD AND WORTHLESS, AND THIS CAN AFFECT ALL THEIR OTHER RELATIONSHIPS.

WE CAN STOP CYBERBULLIES BY BLOCKING OR REPORTING THEM AND BY TELLING AN ADULT ABOUT WHAT IS HAPPENING ONLINE.

Our differences should be celebrated, not bullied. When someone is different, it is easy to think that you know what they are like.

But there are many things that make up someone's identity, and it is important to find out about all of them before we **judge** someone.

EMOTIONS IN RELATIONSHIPS

EMOTIONS ARE AN IMPORTANT PART OF OUR IDENTITY AND HOW WE BEHAVE.

Our relationships have a big impact on our emotions and happiness. This is why it is important that we surround ourselves with healthy relationships. When we have a best friend, we feel happy when we spend time around them, and we want to be around them more. However, sometimes we don't get on with people. For example we might not get on with our brother or sister, and if we fight and argue a lot, it can make us feel sad or upset.

DIFFICULT EMOTIONS

It is always OK to feel emotions, whether that is anger, sadness, fear or any other feeling. However, it is not always OK to act on these emotions. Sometimes in a relationship, you might be upset with someone because of something they have done, or because of the way that they act. It is OK to feel like this, but it is important to control your emotions and keep the relationship healthy, fair and safe. We must always think about consent and treat people with respect, even if we are full of difficult emotions.

HANDLING STRONG EMOTIONS

Controlled breathing is a good way to calm down from many emotions. Slow, deep breaths can make you feel less angry or anxious. Next time you need to calm down, try following these steps:

– Breathe in through your nose for five seconds
– Hold your breath for five seconds
– Breathe out through your mouth for five seconds
– Do the steps again until you feel calm

THINK ABOUT THE EMOTIONS THAT YOU WANT TO RELEASE WHILE YOU ARE BEING CREATIVE.

Talking to trusted adults and friends is another good way of releasing emotions. Emotions can also be released by being creative or making something. Next time you need to release emotions, try painting a picture, writing a story or making up a song.

APOLOGISING

If you ever hurt or upset someone, it is important to apologise. Every time we hurt someone, we lose some of the trust and respect in the relationship. To heal the relationship, it is important to apologise and talk about it so it doesn't happen again.

27

SPEAKING OUT

Consent is an important part of a relationship, and it is important to speak to someone if you do not give consent and you are ignored. It can be very upsetting when this happens, and you might not want to tell anybody about it. You might think you are not allowed to tell anybody. However, it is always a good idea to speak up. It will help you feel better, and it will also help the person who ignored you to realise that they did something wrong. They can then change how they behave next time.

SPEAKING OUT ABOUT SOMETHING IS THE BEST WAY TO MAKE A CHANGE.

When people talk about things in the open, it can help others feel comfortable talking about it as well. For example, once someone stands up to a bully, then other people might realise that they are not alone, and stand up to the bully as well. It is much easier to deal with a problem with the support of other people.

PRINCE WILLIAM WORKS WITH HIS CHARITY, THE ROYAL FOUNDATION, TO HELP PEOPLE SPEAK OUT AGAINST BULLYING.

GETTING SUPPORT

If someone does something involving your personal boundaries or your body that makes you uncomfortable, you can tell them to stop because they do not have your consent. If that person ignores you, it is important to talk to a trusted adult. You may want to talk to a parent or carer about what happened. If you feel that you can't talk to your family, try talking to a teacher or the school nurse.

> CHILDLINE IS AN ORGANISATION THAT USES COUNSELLORS TO TALK TO CHILDREN AND TEENAGERS ABOUT THEIR PROBLEMS. CHILDLINE TALK TO PEOPLE ON THE PHONE, THROUGH EMAIL OR IN PERSON. IF YOU LIVE IN THE UK, YOU CAN CALL CHILDLINE ON 0800 1111.

COUNSELLOR

If an adult does something wrong and unsafe to you, even after you've said no, you might see a counsellor. Counsellors are people who are specially trained to help people deal with difficult emotions and feelings. They will listen to you talk about your experience, then decide what to do next. When an adult does something wrong, it is not your fault. A counsellor will help you talk about what happened.

ACTIVITY

HERE ARE SOME QUESTIONS TO DISCUSS WITH THE REST OF YOUR CLASS.

 **1** What are your personal boundaries? What does privacy mean to you?

 **4** If someone doesn't say anything, does that count as consent?

 **2** Can you describe what it means to give consent?

 **5** Can you make a list of all your relationships?

 **3** How would you change a relationship that you felt was unhealthy?

GLOSSARY

affectionate	showing love, usually by physical things such as kissing or hugging
anonymous	when the identity or name of a person isn't known
communicate	pass information between two or more people
connection	a link or a familiar bond between two things or people
conversations	talking between two people
dramatic	made to give an exciting or entertaining effect
favour	doing something kind for someone
genitals	reproductive organs found between the legs that are different for males and females; for males this is the penis and for females it is the vagina
ignored	not listened to or not being given any attention
intimidated	made to feel scared by someone with more power
judge	form an opinion of someone or something
legally	performed within the limits of the law
nauseous	feeling like you need to be sick
personal boundaries	rules that each person makes about what they are comfortable with in relation to privacy, their body and the close space around their body
physical	relating to the body
respect	to consider the feelings, wishes and rights of other people
social	relating to a group of people or a community
support	give help to something or someone else
traditions	beliefs or behaviours that have been passed down from one generation to the next
unrealistic	something that wouldn't commonly be found in the real world
violent	use force to physically hurt someone

INDEX